GW01465377

Secrets
to
Self-Care

Steps to soothe
your mind and body

ALLSORTED.

for all your gift books and gift stationery

This edition first published in Great Britain in 2024
by Allsorted Ltd., WD19 4BG.

All rights reserved. No part of this work may be reproduced
in any form or by any means, electronic or mechanical,
including photocopying, recording or by any information
storage and retrieval system, without the prior written
permission of the publisher.

All information in this publication is for educational and
informational purposes. It is not intended as a substitute
for professional advice. Should you decide to act upon any
information in this publication, you do so at your own risk.
While the information in this publication has been verified to
the best of our abilities, we cannot guarantee that there are
no mistakes or errors.

© Susanna Geoghegan Gift Publishing

Author: Sasha Morton

Illustrator: Jo Parry
Cover and concept design: Jo Parry and Nick Pettit
Contents design: Blackbird Brands

ISBN: 9-781-915902-52-8

Printed in China

10 9 8 7 6 5 4 3 2 1

Introduction

"Self-care: The practice of taking an active role in protecting one's own wellbeing and happiness, in particular during periods of stress."

Oxford English Dictionary

You may have heard the term 'self-care' and thought that it sounds like an excuse to go out for coffee or have an afternoon nap. Well, if that becomes a bright spot in your week, what's wrong with giving it a try? Spending time doing things that bring us happiness can fall by the wayside as we navigate daily life. There's no one form of self-care that has more value than another – whatever makes your mind and body feel refreshed and restored is a self-care win.

This book will guide you towards understanding and developing self-care skills and strategies that will enhance each day. The inspiring quotes, tips, strategies and suggestions will encourage you to find new ways to fill your time and remind you that doing something for yourself is always better than doing nothing.

"The most important
relationship in your life
is the relationship you
have with yourself."

Diane von Fürstenberg

"It's not selfish to love yourself,
take care of yourself,
and to make your happiness
a priority. It's necessary."

Mandy Hale

Your sense of self

Knowing who we are is vital for realising when we might need to pause and take stock of our mental and physical wellbeing. Having a good sense of self makes us aware of when negative or disruptive experiences threaten to derail our equilibrium. It allows us to anticipate problems and set boundaries – which in turn enable us to put mechanisms in place to bring peace and order back to our lives. Having a greater knowledge of who we are means we understand what is important to us and recognise and celebrate our positive qualities.

Who we are as individuals depends on many things – how we were brought up, who we surround ourselves with, and how open we are to reassessing our identity at different points in our lives. Having a solid sense of self is important for nurturing robust, loving relationships; for building a healthy sense of self-esteem; for living an authentic, honest life; and for maintaining a positive outlook. By bringing self-care strategies into this mix, we are forced to slow down, check in with ourselves and make sure we aren't overlooking our personal needs.

"If your compassion does not include yourself, it is incomplete."

Jack Kornfield

"I'VE LEARNT NOT TO TAKE EVERYTHING TOO SERIOUSLY."

Harry Styles

Start with good people

There's nothing more satisfying than a good chat with old friends – those people who know us well enough that no topic is off limits, or if it is, they will understand the reason why. Being comfortable with the people you surround yourself with, or who lift you up if you're feeling low, is an amazing gift! And nurturing those relationships is a testament to the quality of your character and theirs.

However, we probably all have someone in our lives who is more of a drain than a radiator – that person who takes more than they give to the relationship. If you find yourself feeling anxious over seeing or contacting a particular person, it's time to dial down that connection to protect yourself from negative influences or behaviours that make you unhappy. Self-care is about preserving your energy so you stay well – physically, mentally and emotionally. In this spirit, don't be afraid to politely excuse yourself from being around people who bring you down. You don't need to make a big statement over this decision. It can be enough to prioritise those who are good company, or who might be more in need of your support themselves at a particular time.

If you feel comfortable doing so, why not tell your friends or loved ones how much you appreciate them being in your life? Spread the self-care love by boosting their self-esteem, too!

"I noticed every time I felt overwhelmed, I would hold my breath. I had to learn to stop, relax, and take long deep breaths, and within seconds I would feel more clear and ready to deal with the situation in a more loving way."

Gisele Bündchen

"An empty lantern provides no light. Self-care is the fuel that allows your light to shine brightly."

Unknown

Keep calm and carry on

Racing heart, shallow breaths, clammy palms, muscle tension and feelings of dread ... none of these are an uncommon reaction to stress or anxiety, but they contribute towards making us feel overwhelmed. If this happens to you, these self-care coping strategies will help to restore calm to your body and mind.

- Breathe in through your nose for a count of four, hold for a count of four and exhale through your mouth for a count of four.

- If you can, stand near an open window or step outside. Look up at the sky and do the same 4−4−4 breathing technique in the fresh air.

- Explain to a colleague, friend or family member that you might need extra time or additional support to manage what needs to be done.

- If you are at capacity in a particular aspect of your life, don't take on more responsibilities in that area.

Make a list of all the things you need to do and prioritise them – this will help you feel more organised and will give you a plan for moving forwards. Looking critically at your list will empower you to take actions to feel more in control …

🍃 Delete anything on the list that isn't critical or doesn't add value to your day.

🍃 Defer or delegate things that are not time-sensitive or could be done by someone else.

🍃 Do what you can and be kind to yourself. Start with the small tasks and tick them off – visual evidence that you're making progress is always positive!

"The challenge is not
to be perfect,
it's to be whole."

Jane Fonda

"To experience peace does not mean that your life is always blissful. It means that you are capable of tapping into a blissful state of mind amidst the normal chaos of a hectic life."

Jill Bolte Taylor

Let go of negative emotions

It's normal to feel uneasy or upset about things that go wrong, but holding onto negative emotions is a certain way to exhaust your emotional energy. Whether its feeling you've let someone down, or that you've betrayed a confidence, allowing these thoughts to grow out of proportion stops you from either moving on or learning from them. These ideas will help you to step back and regain your emotional equilibrium.

- Identify the emotion and then try to consider it objectively.

- Accept the feeling and write down what you notice about it.

- Give yourself permission to let it go.

- Reward yourself by doing something special or practising an act of self-care that brings you comfort.

🌿 Talk to someone trustworthy who can help reframe this emotion. Let them remind you of all the other things that you should be proud of about yourself.

These affirmations will enable you to bring clarity to your mind afterwards.

🌿 What is done is done.

🌿 I am at peace with myself.

🌿 I am on the right path.

🌿 I embrace the present moment.

🌿 I have a bright future.

"To love oneself is the beginning of a lifelong romance."

Oscar Wilde

"Too many people overvalue what they are not and undervalue what they are."

Malcolm S. Forbes

You do you!

It's easy to fall into the trap of comparing ourselves to other people and to judge our successes in life, work, relationships or fitness against theirs. Comparisons can be a healthy way to explore our position in life, but they can also weaken our identity and make us feel as though we are not valuable individuals in our own right. Making unhealthy comparisons can distract us from achieving our own goals and prompt us to question our values. All that comes from this cycle of doubt is confusion!

If you find yourself falling into a comparison trap, these self-care check-in exercises will help you to reset your thought processes and remind yourself who YOU really are.

1. Reflect on your best qualities – make a list of the characteristics that define you.

2. Keep a gratitude journal.

3. Record your successes, big and small. Whether it's a promotion at work or keeping a plant alive – toot your own horn!

4. Remind yourself that if someone else is doing well it doesn't mean you aren't. Everyone is running their own race.

5. Remember that social media amplifies the good – but it's only an edited highlights reel and doesn't represent anyone's life in its entirety.

6. Smile at yourself in the mirror every morning. Never forget you are one of a kind – and that's a good thing!

"TALK TO
YOURSELF
LIKE YOU
WOULD TO
SOMEONE
YOU LOVE."

Brené Brown

"When we give ourselves
compassion, we are
opening our hearts
in a way that can
transform lives."

Kristen Neff

Trigger issues

Life events happen, and unexpected things can knock us off course, but when people consider what they would most like to improve about their daily lives, very often the same sorts of issues tend to crop up. Instead of dwelling on them, take a step towards a positive reset. These small but motivational acts of self-care will support you in overcoming common difficulties and help to improve your mood!

The problem: Lack of exercise
The solution: Download a fitness app that contains short, guided stretching routines you can carry out each morning before you get going with your day.

The problem: Bad eating habits or food intolerances
The solution: Reduce your dependency on ultra-processed food, or those containing sugar, colourings, preservatives and additives. Aim to keep your diet simple and clean.

The problem: Poor-quality sleep
The solution: Invest in blackout blinds/lined curtains or a weighted blanket, keep your bedroom cool, and turn off digital devices at least an hour before bed.

The problem: Too much to do
The solution: Make a list each evening to 'brain dump' the things you mustn't forget to do tomorrow. If this doesn't bring you relief, write a list of daily achievements – no matter how trivial – before you settle down to sleep so that you end the day in a positive state of mind.

The problem: Stuck in a rut
The solution: Plan a one-off treat or outing – and commit to doing it!

"Don't take your health for granted. Don't take your body for granted. Do something today that communicates to your body that you desire to care for it."

Jada Pinkett Smith

"To keep the body in good health is a duty ... otherwise we shall not be able to keep our mind strong and clear."

Buddha

Get moving

Caring for our bodies is a vital way to ensure we are looking after ourselves now and for the future. A regular, varied and interesting exercise routine* is an act of self-care that will have long-term benefits, not just for our physical health, but for our mental health, too. Mood-boosting endorphins are released by the brain when we exercise, which improves sleep and reduces stress and anxiety. This, in turn, makes us want to repeat this activity! Before you know it, you've formed a feel-good habit that will improve your confidence and sense of wellbeing.

To really feel the benefit, try every day to move your body in a way that makes you breathe faster or feel warmer; whether it's by walking the dog or pushing a lawnmower – all movement counts. And if you struggle to feel motivated, why not join a class or group and make new social connections at the same time? The ideas below may help you begin a lifelong exercise habit.

- T'ai chi
- Yoga
- Pilates
- Swimming
- Walking/hiking
- Dancing
- Cycling
- Running
- Tennis

*Always consult a medical professional before starting a new exercise routine if you have any health concerns or pre-existing health conditions.

"People who love
to eat are always
the best people."

Julia Childs

"Food is the most

primitive form

of comfort."

Sheliah Graham Westbrook

Eat mindfully

Labelling foods as 'good' or 'bad', saying "I shouldn't" or deciding something we enjoy is a 'guilty pleasure' can spoil our attitude towards what we eat. Much of our daily lives revolves around what we are going to shop for, cook and consume. The more we can embrace a flexible, middle ground between overindulgence and calorie control, the more positive our relationship with food will be – and the less anxiety we will have about our overall diet.

Mindful eating is about both considering what we eat, and being attentive to how much enjoyment we take from it. Savouring the smells, flavours and textures of food – and focusing on these while we eat – is a start. Concentrating on what is in every single mouthful may not be realistic, but pacing yourself as you eat will make you feel more satisfied.

Putting down your devices while you eat will also enable you to register when you've had enough – and make you less likely to reach for the snacks later on!

Rely on your intuition over portion sizes and the times of your meals – and don't beat yourself up if you overindulge from time to time. Reframing your relationship with food to reduce guilt and develop positive associations with food is an act of self-care which, once learned, is a hard habit to break.

"One cannot think well,
love well, sleep well,
if one has not dined well."

Virginia Woolf

"Food is love made visible."

Sarah Ban Breathnach

Mood-boosting food

When you need to boost your mood, these healthy feel-good foods will give your mind and body just what they deserve. Bon appétit!

🌿 **Green tea:** Contains L-theanine, which relaxes the mind while improving concentration and focus.

🌿 **Spinach:** Packed with iron, as well as magnesium and calcium to calm the nervous system.

🌿 **Pumpkin seeds:** A source of magnesium and zinc, which stabilises blood sugar levels.

🌿 **Salmon, tuna, eggs, mushrooms:** Full of vitamin D to maintain healthy teeth, bones and muscles, and stave off low mood during the winter months.

🌿 **Avocado:** An all-rounder that benefits the heart, digestion, mood and balances hormones.

🌿 **Bananas, chicken, turkey:** Full of the amino acid

tryptophan, which increases melatonin levels in the brain to regulate sleep.

🌿 **Oats:** A wholegrain carb that releases its energy slowly, which avoids spikes in blood-sugar levels.

🌿 **Beans and lentils:** An excellent source of B vitamins, these powerhouse proteins contain zinc, magnesium and selenium. They also increase levels of neurotransmitters in the brain, such as dopamine and serotonin, which improve mood.

🌿 **Blueberries and grapes:** Packed with mood-improving antioxidants. Some studies have shown that eating a diet high in fruit and vegetables can reduce incidences of depression.

And finally, scientific research in the US has also concluded that a single glass of wine can act as an antidepressant. Cheers!

"Self-care is not selfish.

You cannot serve from

an empty vessel."

Eleanor Brownn

"MUSIC GIVES A SOUL
TO THE UNIVERSE,
WINGS TO THE MIND,
FLIGHT TO THE
IMAGINATION, AND LIFE
TO EVERYTHING."

Plato

The magic of music

Listening to music is a wonderful way to connect to other people, times and places – and it's one of the most powerful ways we can tap into our emotions. Research has shown that when we listen to music, the regions in the brain responsible for processing sound, memory and emotion become engaged. That sense of nostalgia you get when you hear a dance-floor classic from your college years or the first dance at a wedding? The science confirms this isn't a coincidence –music releases endorphins that make us feel uplifted or happy.

Spend a self-care session curating a perfect playlist and you'll be able to enjoy the soundtrack to your life whenever you feel like it. Music streaming apps, such as Spotify, contain almost every song you can think of, and as you go on a musical scavenger hunt to find old favourites, you're sure to come across some new discoveries as well. Why not set up a selection of playlists to suit your mood, activity or time of day, such as for:

- workout/running

- calming/relaxing

- work/commuting

- cleaning the house

- getting ready to go out

- winding down before bed.

Podcasts, concerts, audiobooks and radio stations are also a great way to discover new listening material. The more you use streaming apps, the more content tailored to your preferences will be offered, so use the technology to build a library of sound into which you can escape!

"The thing that is really
hard, and really amazing,
is giving up on being perfect
and beginning the work
of becoming yourself."

Anna Quindlen

"Self-care is not
a waste of time.
Self-care makes
your use of time
more sustainable."

Jackie Viramontez

Self-care activities 1

If you like your self-care to be more analogue than digital, here are some ideas for things to occupy your mind without needing to look at a screen.

Visit a museum or gallery: Many large towns or cities have a museum or gallery containing national or regional displays or artwork of interest. Pop-up exhibitions in town halls or college/university graduate exhibitions are also worth checking out. The calming environment can promote relaxation, and you may find creative inspiration for your own artistic endeavours.

Take a trip to your local library: As well as offering a wide selection of reading material for adults, going to the library with children is a great way to occupy their time and take advantage of new books and resources to enjoy together. The more people use libraries, the more likely they are to survive – you might even find like-minded individuals running groups or activities there for you or your family to participate in.

Play a board game or go to a quiz night: Organising a games night with friends or family is a great way to bond without having to keep conversations going! Playing games or taking part in a quiz brings out everyone's competitive nature – and you may learn something too!

"Invent your world.
Surround yourself with
people, colour, sounds,
and work that nourish you."

Susan Ariel Rainbow Kennedy (SARK)

"You can't use up creativity.
The more you use,
the more you have."

Maya Angelou

Get creative

Creative activities can provide a sense of fulfilment and purpose, boost self-esteem and generate a sense of contentment and achievement. Dedicating time to something you're interested in is a definite self-care win – especially if you can make this a regular date with yourself. In fact, many psychologists think that taking time to be creative is as important to our mental and physical health as food, meditation and exercise. It gives us permission to focus on one thing at a time, and to exist 'in the moment' rather than juggling different tasks.

Take time to work out what creative activity will suit you best. The greatest benefits are to be gained by doing something you genuinely want to spend time doing – rather than it being another item on your 'to-do' list and feeling like a chore. Many of the following activity ideas are easy to get underway with a guided kit or online instruction videos. Online resource hubs, such as Domestika, offer tutorials to get inspired with an expert by your side. Alternatively, you could sign up to a dedicated group for tuition and to meet people with shared skills and interests.

- Knitting, crochet, cross stitch, quilting or embroidery – start with a guided kit and look for instruction videos online to learn any techniques you need.

- Painting, sketching, mindful colouring, photography, calligraphy.

- Bullet journaling, scrapbooking, creative writing.

- Candle-making, sculpting, pottery, miniature model-building, jewellery-making.

- Cookery, baking, cookie and cake decorating.

"Breathe. Let go.

And remind yourself

that this very moment

is the only one you

know you have for sure."

Oprah Winfrey

"Life should be touched,
not strangled. You've got
to relax, let it happen
at times, and at others
move forward with it."

Ray Bradbury

Slow down

"More haste, less speed."
"Slow down to speed up."
"Stop the world, I want to get off!"

The pace of everyday life is often draining – and rushing through the day can lead to making mistakes or hasty decisions that you regret later. These top tips for living more slowly will help you to take back control of a racing mind or aching body.

Practise meditation: Meditation will help to reduce stress and increase focus. If you need guidance, try using a meditation app such as Calm.

Turn your phone to silent: This will enable you to concentrate on completing a task without interruption.

Make a space that you can retreat to: If your circumstances allow, find a quiet place in your home or garden in which you can spend a few moments to regroup on a busy day. Treat this as a hideaway which only has the purpose of being somewhere you go to relax.

Take a break: Taking regular breaks during work is beneficial to your productivity and your body. If you spend time sitting, try doing a Pilates roll-down or stretch out your lower back and hips in child's pose.

Rest your eyes: To reduce the chance of eye strain, and to help you refocus, take a screen break every 20 minutes, for 20 seconds, while looking at something 20 feet away.

Focus on being present in the moment: Look closely at something, listen to the sound of the world around you, hold an object and concentrate on how it feels to the touch.

"Love yourself first,
and everything else
falls into line."

Lucille Ball

"Be patient with yourself.
Self-growth is tender;
it's holy ground. There's
no greater investment."

Stephen Covey

Wellbeing check-in

When were you last kind to yourself?

Demonstrating self-compassion has many benefits, including boosting self-esteem and improving resilience. When you are feeling despondent, imagine what you would say to make someone feel uplifted or encouraged, and then reframe those words and phrases to demonstrate kindness to yourself.

When did you last practise gratitude?

Taking time to practise gratitude can help to reduce anxiety and improve mood. To put you into a positive mindset, try to notice and appreciate the little things in life that bring you satisfaction. Write them down or make a mental note of them.

When did you last help someone else?

When we help others, it improves the way we feel about

ourselves and can even improve our physical health. Small acts of kindness have reciprocal benefits, as well as activating areas of the brain associated with social connections and trust.

What can you let go of?

Don't be fearful of decluttering your mind, home or relationships of toxic or negative elements. Once you get into the habit of letting go of things that no longer bring you happiness, you'll feel unburdened and less inclined to repeat the same mistakes.

How can you reframe your thoughts?

Allow yourself to accept negative thoughts, but then actively focus on ways to turn them into positive ones and stop dwelling on what you can't control.

"KEEP GOOD
COMPANY, READ
GOOD BOOKS,
LOVE GOOD
THINGS AND
CULTIVATE SOUL
AND BODY AS
FAITHFULLY
AS YOU CAN."

Louisa May Alcott

"Whatever you are doing,
love yourself for doing it.
Whatever you are feeling,
love yourself for
feeling it."

Thaddeus Golas

Eight reasons to relax with a good book

It might already be one of your most trusted sources of entertainment, but if it isn't yet on your self-care agenda, here are some scientifically backed reasons why reading is extraordinarily good for you!

- Reading helps you relax, and regular reading sessions can lower blood pressure and reduce stress.

- Reading makes you more empathetic – by experiencing a range of emotions through reading, you build the ability to deal with challenging situations and develop your own resilience.

- Reading connects you to other cultures, lifestyles, perspectives and experiences.

- Reading before bed helps you get to sleep (as long as it's a printed book and not a tablet or e-reader device) and promotes better-quality sleep.

🍃 Reading increases your knowledge and vocabulary, as well as critical-thinking skills and creativity.

🍃 Reading can boost your brainpower by improving memory function. This staves off cognitive decline, which can reduce your chance of developing diseases such as Alzheimer's.

🍃 Reading fills your imagination and transports you to another world when the real one wears you down.

🍃 Reading brings people together – reading aloud, sharing recommendations in real life and online, going to a book group or connecting to other book lovers through social media … there's no downside to being a reader!

"... replace your vicious stress cycle with a vicious cycle of self-care."

Dr Sara Gottfried

"Sometimes the most important thing in a whole day is the rest we take between two deep breaths ..."

Etty Hillesum

Remind yourself to breathe

Yawning more than usual? Grinding your teeth at night? Struggling with tight neck and shoulder muscles? Sighing more deeply than usual? If you find yourself experiencing any of these physical symptoms, take some time to train yourself to breathe deeply. Breathing effectively makes sure your respiratory and lymphatic systems are working optimally, reduces sensations of nervousness or anxiety, and releases toxins and muscle tension. Try the following exercises to help reap the benefits of deep breathing.

- Breathe in and out through the nose, not through the mouth.

- Focus on getting your breath to move fully from your diaphragm, not your chest. You should feel or sense your belly rise before your ribs if you are inhaling correctly.

Exhaling for a little longer than you inhale activates the parasympathetic nervous system – the part of the network of nerves that relax the body after it has experienced a period of stress.

Set aside five minutes each day to lie down and focus on your breath.

If you struggle to get to sleep, focus on the rhythm of your breath. Breathe in for a count of five, hold for a count of five, then exhale slowly for a count of 10. Repeat until you feel comfortably relaxed.

"Learning to love yourself

is like learning to walk

– essential, life-changing, and

the only way to stand tall."

Vironika Tugaleva

"Quiet the mind,

and the soul will speak."

Ma Jaya Sati Bhagavati

Candle meditation for beginners

"Meditate: Focus one's mind for a period of time, either for spiritual purposes or as a method of relaxation."

Oxford English Dictionary

Meditation is a technique for focusing and calming the mind. It is something that appears easy – but being relaxed in a moment while also being attentive to a focus, such as a sensation or sound, can seem counter-intuitive! The aim is to come away from your meditation feeling refreshed, but it might take a while to find a technique that works for you. However, it's well worth having the ability to meditate in your self-care support kit, and candle meditation is a good place to start your practice.

1. Place a lit candle on a low surface that is at your eye level when you are sitting straight-backed and cross legged on the floor in front of it.

2. Relax your muscles and slowly breathe in and out through your nose, making sure your breath reaches your diaphragm.

3. Look at the flame of the candle for as long as you can without blinking, then close your eyes and visualise the flame in your mind. Hold this image for as long as you can.

4. Once you lose the image, follow steps 2 and 3 again. If thoughts appear in your mind, just let them drift by without focusing on them.

5. Carry on this meditation for as long as you wish (but for at least three minutes), then blow out the candle and rest before returning to your day in the spirit of renewal.

"Almost everything will
work again if you unplug
it for a few minutes,
including you."

Anne Lamott

"The quiet mind is

richer than a crown."

Robert Greene

Digital detox

We've all been there – mindlessly checking our phones while watching TV or losing hours in an online shopping rabbit hole when we could be doing something more productive! Not only does this overload our brains with information that we often don't need, scrolling becomes an addictive habit as every new notification triggers a tiny release of the neurotransmitter dopamine. This prompts us to take action, driving us into a cycle of response and react instead of being in control of our own digital existence.

It can also be easy to feel as though our world only exists through our devices. Keeping in touch with people through social media can be hugely rewarding, but it can lead to neglect of relationships in real life. Negative influences and a loss of perspective, or focusing on misleading or toxic messages, can be problematic, too. So, what can you do? A self-care digital detox will help you to focus on real-life relationships, reduce stress and regain perspective. Here are some tips to get you started.

Set a daily screen time limit through your smartphone's settings or via an app.

Reduce your dependence on social media or games by listening to podcasts, music or audiobooks.

Leave your devices in a different room when you are doing something else so that this activity has your sole focus.

Allocate specific time slots to reply to messages and posts, then turn off notifications or put your phone on silent/airplane mode).

Put your 'out of office' response on so colleagues know you won't be responding to emails out of working hours

"Carve out and claim
the time to care for
yourself and kindle
your own fire."

Amy Ippoliti

"WHEN YOU CAN'T FIND YOUR PURPOSE IN A DAY, MAKE IT TO LOOK AFTER YOURSELF."

Dodie Clark

Create a routine

While some people crave unpredictability and thrive on seeing where the day takes them, for others this can create a sense of stress and loss of control. Having a routine can really help with self-care by enabling us to avoid procrastination and to feel a sense of achievement about organising our time effectively.

Your routine will be very personal to you, but making a list of daily tasks and putting them in order of importance is a good way to start! By breaking down your day into productive time slots, you will probably find there are some tasks you could do less frequently or in a more organised way, such as the laundry or food shopping, leaving more time for self-care activities, such as reading or exercising. Repetition of non-negotiable tasks – school runs, for example – are inevitable, but managing your day to tackle the jobs that require the most energy when you are feeling most alert will help define its structure. You should also factor in regular breaks, make sure you eat and stay hydrated.

Review your routine after a month. By then you should know if it has alleviated any stress or anxiety. Revise as required – and don't be afraid to let some spontaneity creep in, too!

"Resting is a part of
the process, even if it's
not a part of the plan."

Carley Schweet

"If you get tired,

learn to rest, not to quit."

Banksy

Managing sleep

The blue light emitted by the screens on our smartphones, computers, TVs and devices tricks our brains into thinking it should stop making melatonin, the hormone that helps us sleep. Try these tips to create a sleep plan to optimise your wellbeing. It will reap self-care dividends – but be patient: it takes around two months for a new routine to become an established habit.

- **Decide on a bedtime and wake-up time:** Our body clock craves routine, so try to stick as close to this as you can at weekends or on days off, too. (Although an occasional lie-in is perfectly acceptable!)

- **Make your bedroom sleep-friendly:** Invest in black-out blinds or lined curtains; set the temperature so that you can sleep comfortably (cooler is better than too warm); consider buying a light-based or controllable alarm clock that wakes you gradually; keep screens turned off or leave them outside the room.

Get into relaxation mode: Your body starts making melatonin at around 8pm. Turn off devices or change them to a red-light setting from this time. Do anything that helps you feel more prepared to wind down, such as getting your bag/clothing ready for the next day or having a relaxing shower or bath. Try to keep to the same routine so that your brain and body learn that this is what happens before going to sleep.

Don't force it: If sleep doesn't come naturally once you get into bed, get up and do something relaxing in a different space until you feel tired enough to try again. Read a book, have a hot drink, listen to some calming music ... encourage yourself to only associate your bed with sleep.

Assess and adjust: Tweak timings, routines and relaxation methods until you get your sleep routine right.

"But when I take the time to take care of myself, to go to the doctor, go to a spa, get a deep-tissue massage, get adjusted by a chiropractor ... I feel I can face life with a renewed vigor and renewed passion."

Viola Davis

"Being comfortable in your own skin is one of the most important things to achieve. I'm still working on it!"

Kate Mara

Aromatherapy

"Aromatherapy: The use of aromatic plant extracts and essential oils for healing and cosmetic purposes."

Oxford English Dictionary

Feel as though you could benefit from some soothing scent-based TLC? Aromatherapy can be great for self-care as a way to boost your mood, bring calm to your day or help you sleep. To make your own blend to apply to your skin, dilute 12 drops of your chosen essential oil in a carrier oil such as almond, olive or jojoba. Massage onto your temples, wrists, or soles of the feet. These are the main properties of some of the most popular aromatherapy fragrances.

🌿 **Chamomile** brings calm.

🌿 **Grapefruit** energises and detoxifies.

🌿 **Rosemary** boosts circulation.

🌿 **Juniper** reduces fluid retention.

🌿 **Geranium** balances hormones.

- **Lavender** eases aches and pains.

- **Rose** boosts mood.

- **Frankincense** focuses the mind.

- **Bergamot orange** reduces anxiety.

- **Ginger** aids digestion.

- **Lemongrass** brings clarity.

- **Tea tree** deodorises and reduces feelings of stress.

- **Eucalyptus and pine** decongests a blocked nose, alleviates seasonal allergies.

Always use essential oils carefully; although they are natural products, they can cause adverse reactions if not used correctly. Make sure the essential oils you are using do not conflict with any medication you may be taking, and always check it's safe to use them if you are pregnant. To get the best out of your aromatherapy experience, it's best to talk to a qualified aromatherapist or healthcare professional first

"We cannot direct
the wind, but we can
adjust the sails."

Dolly Parton

"KEEP FEEDING YOURSELF WITH POSITIVITY."

Iman Shumpert

The power of crystals

Whether you believe in the healing power of crystals or not, these beautiful stones have become more commonly available in recent years. For some, wearing or holding stones that work with the invisible energy sources in the body, called chakras, are vital to influence change and bring about a sense of calm or relief. Crystals can be worn as jewellery, carried in a pocket or bag, or kept as an ornament to enhance a room's atmosphere. Perhaps one of these could become part of your self-care toolkit?

Clear quartz: If you only choose one crystal to draw healing power from, this is the most versatile of them all. It is believed to cleanse, energise and restore.

Rose quartz: This crystal can help to reduce stress, improve circulation and ease headaches.

Amethyst: Place it under your pillow to improve sleep quality and relieve insomnia.

🌿 **Black tourmaline:** This crystal helps to absorb negative energy.

🌿 **Lapis lazuli:** Often warn as jewellery, lapis lazuli can aid concentration.

🌿 **Citrine:** Place this yellow quartz stone in sunlight to boost your energy and achieve your dreams.

🌿 **Turquoise:** This blue gemstone contains copper, which can benefit aching joints.

🌿 **Amber:** Amber is thought to be beneficial in bringing comfort to those suffering from digestive disorders.

🌿 **Red jasper:** This gemstone can help boost energy levels, stamina and strength.

"A good foot massage
is like a peaceful oasis
in the middle of
a chaotic day."

Unknown

"Your time is limited,
so don't waste it living
someone else's life."

Steve Jobs

Be your own reflexologist

"Reflexology: A system of massage used to relieve tension and treat illness, based in the theory that there are reflex points on the feet, hands and head linked to every part of the body."

Oxford English Dictionary

Learning how to give yourself a mini-reflexology treatment makes for a simple sleep-inducing self-care strategy to fit in before bed, especially if you've spent a lot of time on your feet!

1. Start by sitting comfortably in a quiet space, and using a light, grease-free lotion, massage your feet with kneading, squeezing and stroking actions.

2. Cross your right foot over your left knee and hold your ankle firmly. Place your left thumb on the sole of your foot and inch your thumb firmly from the base of your heel to each toe, pressing firmly. Then apply gentle pressure all around each toe using the side of your thumb or forefinger to release tension throughout the body.

3. Press your thumb into the area of your foot between the pads under your toes, approximately in line with your middle toe. Skim down the whole foot with light 'breeze' strokes to finish. Swap and repeat with the other foot. Then relax!

Learn more by looking at reflexology charts online that identify each part of the foot and how it connects to a different place in the body.

Drinking water after any reflexology actions will help to flush away toxins released during the treatment.

"You aren't doing 'nothing'
when you choose to put
your wellbeing first.
In fact, this is the key
to having everything."

Brittany Burgunder

"Sometimes I give myself
a break. So I will retreat
a moment from the fray,
just to breathe."

Michelle Obama

Just do nothing!

Did you know, the Dutch have a term for the act of doing absolutely nothing? They call this concept *niksen* – and the author of a book on the topic, Olga Mecking, defines it as 'to do nothing, without a purpose'. Mecking explains that this is a reaction to modern living as much as anything else. Because there are so many things that people can do, they fill their time and end up living at a pace that becomes hard to keep up with. As a result, they dream of having more relaxation time and the capacity to do nothing when they embark on it.

Mecking also recommends letting go of the idea that every action needs to have a defined outcome, such as eating a prescribed amount of fruit and vegetables, or walking to achieve a certain number of steps in a day. When you *niksen*, you don't have an end goal in mind for your activity, you just do nothing, without needing to fulfil an objective. If this resonates with you, perhaps it's time to fit in some self-care *niksen*, too!

"Self-care is the number one solution to helping somebody else. If you are being good to yourself and your body and your psyche, that serves other people better because you will grow strong enough to lift someone else up."

Mary Lambert

"Every one of us needs
to show how much
we care for each other
and, in the process,
care for ourselves."

Princess Diana

Self-care with a friend

You might find you are more motivated to practise self-care when you are with a friend. Committing to a regular time slot and having an activity partner means you're less likely to make an excuse to bail out – and some things are just more fun when you have company! That said, if you have a good reason to miss a session or need some time to yourself, give one another the necessary space.

🌿 **Join a class or club:** Swimming, hiking, Pilates, life drawing, spinning, pottery, learning a new skill or language ... just make sure you both have the same level of enthusiasm for whatever you sign up for.

🌿 **Train for something:** A park run, charity marathon or jigsaw puzzle competition ... the friends that train together, slay together!

Volunteer: Not only a great way to connect socially with each other, but in volunteering, you'll be benefiting other people, too.

Diarise a regular walk, cycle or run: Use the time as a mental reset for yourself and to check-in on each other's wellbeing.

Eat together: Set up a regular date to either cook for each other or eat out. If evenings are tricky to make work, a weekend brunch or breakfast date is a great alternative. If all else fails, a quick coffee or glass of wine is better than nothing and shows you are dedicated to maintaining that friendship.

"ADOPT THE PACE OF NATURE: HER SECRET IS PATIENCE."

Ralph Waldo Emerson

"Nature is not a place to visit, it is home."

Gary Snyder

Get outdoors

Nature is one of the best self-care resources there is, and having access to it is one of the most effective ways to improve our mental and physical health – but we all need to work with what's available to us. You may be lucky enough to live near a beach or woodland, with acres of space to explore, but spending time in a park, village green or in your own garden can be just as rewarding. The main thing is to connect with the outdoor world and make the most of what you can see, hear, touch and sense around you.

Time outdoors can be spent profitably to revive and refresh you. Try these self-care ideas to boost your wellbeing!

- Exercise, stretch or practise meditation in the natural environment.

- Breathe deeply and mindfully.

- Learn about nature – take inspiration from the things you see growing around you to do your own planting. Take photographs of interesting plants and flowers, and use a plant finder app to identify them!

- Sketch, draw or photograph what you see and create a scrapbook or album of favourite pieces and pictures.

- Explore somewhere new – you could even borrow a dog from a friend or neighbour to get a different experience of being outdoors.

"Use your smile to change the world; don't let the world change your smile."

Chinese proverb

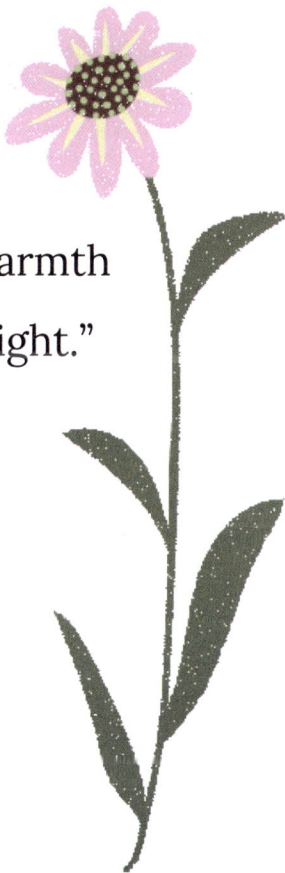

"Bask in the warmth

of your own light."

Amy Perez

Relaxation tips

Relaxation is an important part of the self-care toolkit! It's a great way to de-stress and to calm down. Set a relaxation reminder on your phone – and make sure it's for a time when you can consciously put down what you are doing and focus on being fully immersed in your self-care moment! Here are a few ideas to help you relax.

🌿 Carry out a mindful meditation or breathing exercise using an app, such as Calm.

🌿 Let your imagination wander or listen to classical or relaxing music.

🌿 Watch ASMR (autonomous sensory meridian response) videos. These videos – where gentle sound effects, like whispering and rainfall, or actions, like cutting through soap and raking sand – can have a de-stressing effect on our minds and prompt our brains to release hormones that help us relax, such as dopamine, oxytocin and serotonin.

- Soak in a bath filled with magnesium-rich salts, which, when absorbed into the body through the skin, can elevate serotonin levels. This can increase feelings of calm and help to de-stress the mind and body to improve your mood.

- Drink herbal tea, such as lavender, chamomile, verbena, lemon balm or passionflower, to help you relax and unwind.

"I need to feel like
I've escaped the day
when I get home."

Bella Heathcote

"I have a lovely bathtub that feels like my sanctuary. I fill it up with a lavender bubble bath, read a magazine and just chill out."

Lisa Haydon

Create your own sanctuary

One of the most effective places to relax and unwind is in the comfort of your own home. Even if you don't have the luxury of decorating your entire house to suit your personal preferences and taste, curating an area that is yours alone – for relaxation, at certain times of the day – is a satisfying self-care project.

Start by thinking about the space you have available and how you want to use it. Will it be a reading nook or a meditation zone? Somewhere to do crafting or to write your own lifestyle blog? Think about the furnishings you need, what you can repurpose from elsewhere in the home, and anything you'll need to store away in between uses.

Make sure the chair or seating you use is fit for purpose – there's no benefit in being uncomfortable! – and that the lighting is suitable. The more natural light you can incorporate the better, as the more vitamin D we take in from exposure to sunlight, the more mood-improving serotonin and melatonin we produce. A blind or curtains to create a more cosy or private space if you are doing yoga or meditating, and candles or dimmable/soft bulb lamps will let you control this. A rug will soften hard floors and a relaxing fragrance diffuser will help create atmosphere. Now all you have to do is sit down and relax!

"There is nothing like

staying at home

for real comfort."

Jane Austen

"The light is what guides
you home, the warmth
is what keeps you there."

Ellie Rodriguez

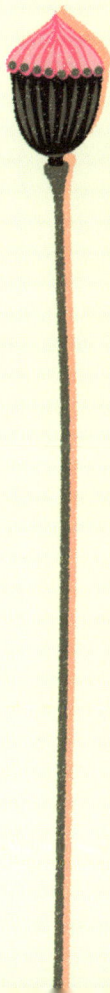

Tidy home, tidy mind

To feel happy in your own environment, there's nothing like a good declutter. Put yourself back in control of your personal spaces with these top tips.

- Once you start decluttering, it will get worse before it gets better! This is all part of the process, so don't get overwhelmed. Keep the end goal in sight and press on!

- Sort out one room or type of item – such as toys, books, clothing, kitchen cupboards – at a time, and have a system in place so you know where the overspill is going. Have strong bags or boxes ready, and organise them by charity shop donation, regifting/passing on/selling and things to take to the recycling centre. Aim to get things out of your home as promptly as you can.

Communicate to everyone you live with what you are doing – and why. Get permission from them to get rid of the personal items they no longer need, and bear in mind there's a fine line between being ruthless and being uncompromising! However, remind them that if they haven't looked at, used or thought about certain items for years, or they've outgrown them, they don't need them.

Don't hold onto things from a sense of guilt or nostalgia. If something doesn't spark joy when you look at, wear or hold it, let it go.

"Self-care is giving the
world the best of you,
instead of what's left of you."

Katie Reed

"THE WORLD WON'T GET MORE OR LESS TERRIBLE IF WE'RE INDOORS SOMEWHERE WITH A MUG OF HOT CHOCOLATE."

Kamila Shamsie

Micro-decluttering

The fewer micro-distractions you have in your life, the more time you can spend on things you love! Follow these organisational tips as part of your self-care strategy to make each day a little easier to navigate.

Tackle similar jobs at the same time: Set aside a focused 30 minutes to take care of things that fall into the same category, such as personal admin. File paperwork, pay bills, write a shopping list and send birthday cards in one session – and then move on.

Take control of technology 1: Every three months, set aside time to review your tech demands. Cancel unwanted subscriptions, delete apps you no longer use, clean out your inbox and junk mail folders, delete photographs or contacts you don't need, unsubscribe from irrelevant mailing lists, and update the software on your devices.

Take control of technology 2: Allocate specific time slots in the day to check emails or messages – use filters or timers to facilitate this, and stick to it! Make sure banking, gym membership, online booking systems and online grocery shopping are set up on the device you use the most, and passwords are saved to make using them quick and straightforward.

Have a place for everything: Keep the things you use the most – such as keys, charging leads, dog leads – where they are easy to access. Organise similar items so that they are in the same place, for example, all the pens and pencils are in one pot and not six different drawers! Get duplicates of things you use all the time: scissors, tweezers, make-up items, portable chargers. If something belongs in a gym bag, laptop bag or handbag, keep it in there and don't let it loose in the house (and sort out those bags each week while you're at it!).

"The beginning is

always today."

Mary Shelley

"The simpler things are,
the happier they are."

Gwyneth Paltrow

Feel better about the planet

Wanting to reduce our impact on the environment is something many of us have on our consciences. Making sensible choices around the clothing we buy is a good way to reduce our impact on the planet and ensure we feel good about what we wear. Fashion production is a carbon and freshwater process, and when textiles find their way into landfill, they contribute to the contamination of soil and groundwater, generating methane gases as they decompose. So, how can you do your part and feel good about it?

- Recycle unwanted clothing/textiles at recycling centres or through retailer recycling initiatives if they can't be donated to charity or sold on.

- Find a good shoe repairer and resole/reheel your footwear when it shows signs of wear and tear. Leather goods repairers can fix broken bag clasps or straps.

🍃 Make alterations – either yourself or through a tailor – to clothing that no longer fits or needs mending. Replacing buttons, broken zips or repairing damage is invariably cheaper than buying something new.

🍃 Wash your clothing at the lowest effective temperature you can using eco-friendly products.

🍃 Buy from smaller, eco-conscious brands or designers who work with ethical suppliers that invest in low-impact, environmentally friendly production techniques and materials.

🍃 Buy only what you need, and reduce spending with fast-fashion brands so that you value what you own and are invested in looking after it.

"Live for each second

without hesitation."

Elton John

"Life is short, and it

is here to be lived."

Kate Winslet

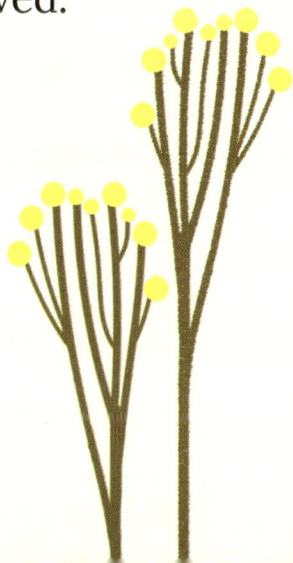

Explore the world

Sometimes, self-care means stepping away from real life and having a complete change of scenery. Even so, we can place a huge amount of pressure on ourselves to plan a perfect getaway. Wherever your travels take you, it's important to try to go with the flow, while ensuring you can still practise your preferred self-care strategies to make the most of your experiences without feeling stressed.

Be open-minded about what you'll get from spending time somewhere new. Use some days for discovery and some for relaxing, and don't feel obliged to pack your itinerary with things other people want to do. If you notice somewhere off the beaten track that you want to explore, go for it! The best way to counteract the essential organisation that travelling entails is to be spontaneous once you're there.

Travelling is also the ideal opportunity to have a digital detox. Immerse yourself in a different landscape, language and culture without feeling the need to record it all or be contactable (unless personal responsibilities demand it). Take this as an opportunity to slow down your pace, clear your head, absorb new sights and sounds, and return home rejuvenated.

"... if you're not comfortable within yourself, you can't be comfortable with others."

Sydney J. Harris

"Who looks outside, dreams; who looks inside, awakes."

Carl Gustav Jung

Gratitude journaling

"Gratitude: The quality of being thankful."

Oxford English Dictionary

Gratitude journaling can help us appreciate all the positive things that occur in our lives. Appreciating simple, uplifting things makes us more empathetic and better at letting go of negative experiences: it's a self-fulfilling self-care strategy!

Add a note in your regular diary or calendar, fill a gratitude box or jar*, or use a ready-made gratitude journal to remind you of something joyful, funny or meaningful that happened during the day. Recording moments of gratitude for people, words or actions takes practice; like any habit, it can take a while to bed in! Don't force it – if you can't think of anything on one day, that's okay.

Here are some examples of things you might feel thankful for.

🌿 I am grateful for my neighbour taking in a parcel.

🌿 I am grateful that the sun shone today.

🌿 I am grateful for my health.

🌿 I am grateful that my children didn't argue today!

🌿 I am grateful for a good night's sleep.

*Write down something you are grateful for on a slip of paper and pop it in a dedicated jar or box each day. Reread them when you need a mood boost!

"Just because there's a hurricane going on around you, doesn't mean you have to open the window and look at it."

Taylor Swift

"Love yourself enough to set boundaries. Your time and energy are precious. You get to choose how you use it."

Anna Taylor

Learn to say "No"

Sometimes, the best thing you can do for yourself is to say no. Most of us are guilty of agreeing to do things we don't have time for, don't want to do, or feel obligated to take on. We feel guilty about letting people down or appearing unhelpful.

As part of your self-care journey, there's no harm in setting boundaries for yourself. The phrases on the right may come in useful when you need to excuse yourself from taking on more than you can manage.

🍃 "I'm sorry, this isn't a good time."

🍃 "I'd love to, but I can't."

🍃 "I'm not actually taking on anything new at the moment."

🍃 "Thanks for thinking of me, but I won't be able to fit it in."

🍃 "Let me get back to you, but it's probably not going to be possible."

🍃 "I'm afraid I can't, but I appreciate being asked."

🍃 "Under different circumstances that would have been great, but I'll have to pass for now."

"Embrace the glorious

mess that you are."

Elizabeth Gilbert

"Sometimes you can't see yourself clearly until you see yourself through the eyes of others."

Ellen DeGeneres

Self-worth tips

Second-guessing yourself? Wallowing in self-doubt? Feeling regretful about how you reacted to a colleague's words or actions? Suffering from imposter syndrome? Everyone experiences a dip in their sense of self-worth from time to time; it's how you handle it that counts! Learning to reflect positively on different situations is a priceless self-care skill.

Don't blame yourself for other people's actions. How they behave in specific situations is on them, not you. Try not to take things said in the heat of the moment or as a quick reaction personally – you never know what is going on in someone else's world at any given time.

Being able to apologise is a valuable quality, but don't apologise for things that aren't your fault. Instead of rushing to say sorry as a default response in an awkward moment, say nothing and see how the situation unfolds.

If other people make you feel belittled or doubtful over your abilities, ask yourself what's the worst that could happen if you asserted yourself. Don't be afraid to speak up and use your voice to challenge inaccurate or unfair assessments. Thought of the perfect response hours later? Put it in an email (it's up to you if you send it) or write it down for another time.

"I've finally stopped running away from myself. Who else is there better to be?"

Goldie Hawn

"Until you value yourself,
you won't value your
time. Until you value
your time, you will not
do anything with it."

M. Scott Peck

Take your time

Life moves increasingly fast, and having the head space to make thoughtful decisions is often the first thing to fall by the wayside. Don't be afraid to slow down. Operating at a slower pace doesn't mean you don't know what you're doing, it just means you want to do things well and not make mistakes. Buy yourself back some mental bandwidth with these self-preservation strategies!

If you've been working flat out on a project, factor in recovery time once it's delivered or keep your email turned off while you catch up. If you can, take a half day off and use it for a self-care catch-up with a favourite activity.

If the day-to-day stress of managing everyone's needs at home falls on you, look for ways to share the responsibility. Use a well-positioned whiteboard or family management app so you don't have to shoulder the mental load of reminding everyone what needs doing or where they need to be!

If you keep forgetting to respond to messages or can't get on top of personal admin, set aside a 'read and reply' session to tackle all your communication tasks in one focused time slot every few days.

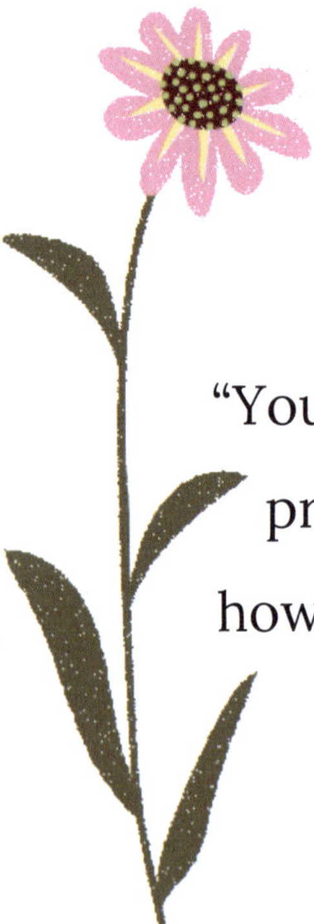

"You are very powerful,
provided you know
how powerful you are."

Yogi Bhajan

"Take care of your body.

It's the only place

you have to live."

Jim Rohn

Tackle your finances

Financial self-care means being able to commit to your outgoings responsibly and not sticking your head in the sand over money concerns. The more you know about your financial position, the more secure you will feel – from filing your tax returns on time to the value of your personal pension.

To help manage your finances, keep a spreadsheet or use an app to record what and when you spend, right down to the last penny. Use what you learn about your spending habits to set a realistic budget for the month – but be realistic about your targets and review your expenditure every few weeks to see where you could make sensible reductions in your outgoings. Arrange an automatic transfer into a savings account as soon as you get paid, and aim to accrue at least three months of salary in savings.

Other financial self-care suggestions include shopping around for better deals on year-round outgoings, such as insurance policies, energy costs and food. Try using comparison websites for ongoing or substantial one-off purchases, and wait for seasonal sales or 'Black Friday' deals for investment items such as tech devices, vehicles or furniture. But remember – taking advantage of a good deal is only worth it if it's for something you really need!

"WHEN YOU RECOVER OR DISCOVER SOMETHING THAT NOURISHES YOUR SOUL AND BRINGS JOY, CARE ENOUGH ABOUT YOURSELF TO MAKE ROOM FOR IT IN YOUR LIFE."

Jean Shinoda Bolen

"So plant your own garden
and decorate your own soul,
instead of waiting for someone
to bring you flowers."

Jorge Luis Borges

Follow your dreams

Don't let self-doubt, overthinking or other people's opinions get in the way of your dreams. A little bit of ground-level spontaneity can lead to bigger and better things. If you want a piercing or a tattoo, get it! If you have the urge to take yourself off on a solo city break, grab your passport and go! If you are naturally cautious, surprise yourself by taking control of your destiny and throwing that caution to the wind. Not only will this self-care surprise boost your confidence and self-esteem, it should prompt other people not to underestimate your zest for life!

Manifestation is the idea that you can think your dream into reality. Why not try it for yourself? All you need is clarity of vision about your objectives and a healthy sense of self-belief. Visualise what you want in as much detail as possible. Think positively about how you could achieve it and the steps you could put into place for it to turn into a tangible outcome. The universe may not provide it for you, but having a strategy and focus can lead to making decisions that set you on the right path to it happening!

"Self-care means
giving yourself
permission to pause."

Cecelia Tran

"Self-care is taking
all the pressures you
are facing right now,
and deciding to which
you will respond, and how."

Imani Shola

The power of colour

If you've ever stepped into a blue-painted room and felt less tense, or received compliments for wearing something in hot pink, you'll have experienced the power of colour. Colour therapists believe that interacting with colours and tones that resonate with your mood or emotions can be an effective self-care strategy, so why not give it a go? Look at some different colours for yourself and pay attention to the feelings that they inspire in you. If blue makes you feel blue or pink makes your heart sink, these aren't the colours for you!

Research suggests that the human brain associates warm colours, such as red, orange and yellow, with feelings of passion, energy, power and anger. Red is believed to stimulate energy and yellow reflects optimism and happiness.

Cooler colours, such as blue, green and purple, create a calming atmosphere, although they can infer indifference or disinterest on an emotional level. Blue implies trust and reliability, while green's associations with the outside world suggests a connection with nature and all things soothingly organic. Surround yourself with colours and tones that make you feel good for a self-care boost!

"Don't sacrifice yourself
too much, because if you
sacrifice too much there's
nothing else you can give
and nobody will care for you."

Karl Lagerfeld

"If you feel burnout
setting in, if you feel
demoralized and exhausted,
it is best, for the sake of
everyone, to withdraw
and restore yourself."

Dalai Lama

Take a moment to relax

The World Health Organization (WHO) defines burnout as 'chronic workplace stress that has not been successfully managed'. In 2019, burnout was included in the WHO's International Classification of Diseases as an occupational phenomenon – and that was before the global workforce navigated the Coronavirus pandemic. If you or your friends and family start to notice any symptoms of burnout (and there are many, ranging from feelings of dread and failure, to physical responses, such as insomnia and headaches), you should take steps to address the situation as quickly as possible. The following self-care measures are a good place to begin.

* First of all, recognise that there is a problem. Speak to your manager or HR department and explain how you feel so that they can offer regular check-ins and support.

- Take a step back from extra-curricular responsibilities. Learn to say no, set realistic goals and stop striving towards unattainable targets.

- Prioritise rest and healthy eating, take regular breaks and aim to fit in 30–60 minutes of exercise daily. Check in with your feelings regularly to evaluate whether the changes you've instigated have improved the situation or if there is more work to do.

- Consider making an appointment with your GP if burnout symptoms continue to an unmanageable degree.

"Allow yourself the things
you need right now.
Whether that's space,
rest, support, or something
else, know that you are
not a burden for taking
care of yourself."

@TWLOHA (X/Twitter)

"TAKE TIME
FOR SELF,
FOR THE
SPIRITUAL,
WITHOUT
FEELING
GUILTY OR
SELFISH."

Beyoncé

Scrapbooking for self-care

Want to find a way into developing your creative skills, but not sure where to begin? Scrapbooking can be an effective self-care pursuit to help you relax, express yourself and reduce anxiety. It is a very individual activity – you choose what you want to put into your scrapbook (a largeish notebook or sketchpad) based on your interests or available materials.

Some people use them to collect and collate memories by bringing together photographs, cuttings and personal souvenirs from different times of their lives. Others use a scrapbook as a physical 'Pinterest board' or way of keeping visual materials – such as magazine images, printouts, labels, postcards, badges, ribbon or stamps – that represent a topic they are interested in or to provide inspiration for an upcoming event. Whatever your theme, the process of gathering, organising, cutting and sticking is a happily mindful self-care activity! Using your hands and testing out new arrangements doesn't require any particular skill – only patience and the ability to recognise when something looks just right and can be stuck into place!

This relaxing and de-stressing self-care activity can also fit easily into any small gaps in your day. You can even do it online if you prefer – search for 'online scrapbooking' and put all those random photos and screenshots on your smartphone to good use.

"Self-care should move you toward a life you don't need to run away from."

Rina Raphael

"Closing your eyes
and listening to silence
is self-care."

Maxime Lagacé

Mindfulness

"Mindfulness: A mental state achieved by focusing one's awareness on the present moment, while calmly acknowledging and accepting one's feelings, thoughts, and bodily sensations."

Oxford English Dictionary

Mindful colouring is an easy way to tap into mindfulness by encouraging you to slow down, move away from a screen and be creative. Pick an adult colouring book that suits your interest, from pop culture to complex mandalas. Gradually seeing a black and white page bloom into colour, while paying attention to the sensation of your pencil on paper, allows for a focused creative meditation.

🍃 **Mindful walking** prompts you to notice the smells, sights and sounds around you as go on a walk. Think about the feel of the ground beneath your feet, the breeze on your skin, the chirping of birds or the rustle of grass. Focus on each step and breath as you move. If you find your mind becoming distracted, pause and bring your attention back to something you can see, touch or smell.

🍃 **Mindful meditation** is when you sit quietly and pay attention to your thoughts, breathing, or the feeling of your body or environment in the moment. Incorporating yoga or breathing exercises into your mindful meditation practice can help calm the mind and provide a valuable opportunity for self-reflection and self-care.

"Caring for your body, mind, and spirit is your greatest and grandest responsibility. It's about listening to the needs of your soul and then honoring them."

Kristi Ling

"Make the most of today.

Get interested in something.

Shake yourself awake.

Develop a hobby.

Let the winds of enthusiasm

sweep through you.

Live today with gusto."

Dale Carnegie

Self-care activities 2

Here are some more self-care suggestions to help stimulate and refresh you.

Drive without a destination: Turn up the music and see where the road takes you. Not a driver? Jump on a train to somewhere you've never been before or get off the bus a few stops earlier and wander around a different neighbourhood. Try to make sure you aren't in a hurry to get back home so you can relax into exploring this new place or space.

Cook something just for you: Find a new recipe that you like the look of, or prepare a forgotten favourite.

Block out time to make your dish without the pressure of feeding other people. Enjoy being able to spend time planning, prepping and cooking – focus on how it looks, tastes and smells, and savour each mouthful.

Rest and let your mind drift: Find a place where you can make yourself comfortable and feel safe and at ease. If you can, being outdoors on a sunny day to take advantage of a vitamin D hit makes this self-care undertaking even more beneficial*. Once you are settled, let your thoughts drift, and sit peacefully in your own company to relax your body and mind.

* Remember to wear sunscreen to protect your skin!

"As you grow older, you will discover that you have two hands: one for helping yourself, the other for helping others."

Maya Angelou

"My mother is a big believer in being responsible for your own happiness. She always talked about finding joy in small moments and insisted that we stop and take in the beauty of an ordinary day."

Jennifer Garner

Seek out inspiration

Not everyone can achieve fame and fortune, but with a little self-belief we can achieve our goals and dreams. To get yourself on the right path, seek out your own inspirational role model and, when you have moments of doubt, let their words deliver a self-belief boost. Reading biographies, articles, blogs and news stories about people who truly know themselves is a great way to take stock of what you value. Here are some wise words from people who knew that by trusting yourself and digging deep into your reserves of inner strength, you can go a long way.

"If you can't fly then run, if you can't run then walk, if you can't walk then crawl, but whatever you do you have to keep moving forwards."

Martin Luther King Jr

"A hero is an ordinary individual who finds the strength to persevere and endure in spite of overwhelming obstacles."

Christopher Reeve

"You're braver than you believe, stronger than you seem, and smarter than you think."

Winnie the Pooh (A.A. Milne)

"Above all, be the heroine of your life, not the victim."

Nora Ephron

"Knowing what must be done does away with fear."

Rosa Parks

"A healthy self-love means we have no compulsion to justify to ourselves or others why we take vacations, why we sleep late, why we buy new shoes, why we spoil ourselves from time to time. We feel comfortable doing things which add quality and beauty to life."

Andrew Matthews

"Work hard.

Play hard.

Be Kind."

Harry Styles

Treat yourself!

While it's important to have plans and goals to aspire to, those little moments of pleasure we find in the day can have just as important an impact on our wellbeing. Here are a few self-care suggestions that may help buoy you up and invigorate you to take on your other challenges!

- Go to the cinema in the middle of the day.

- Buy flowers for yourself.

- Binge-watch a new TV series, or revisit an old favourite.

- Feed the ducks!

- Visit a patisserie and choose an exquisitely delicious cake or chocolates for your consumption only!

- Research upcoming concerts or events – and commit to going (even if it's a solo outing).

🍃 Plan or book a holiday or minibreak.

🍃 Book a table at somewhere you've had on your 'must visit' list for dinner.

🍃 Invest in a good quality coffee machine and have café-style drinks at home.

🍃 Collect paint samples and catalogues, and make a mood or Pinterest board for a fantasy home makeover.

🍃 Research the perfect home fragrance and spritz it around generously.

🍃 Take a spontaneous day off work.

🍃 Have an afternoon power nap.

🍃 Light the candle you've been saving for best!

"Radical self-care is the secret
of joy, resistance and freedom.
When we care for ourselves
as our very own beloved
– with naps, healthy food,
clean sheets, a lovely cup
of tea – we can begin to give
in wildly generous ways to the
world, from abundance."

Anne Lamont

"Beauty begins the
moment you decide
to be yourself."

Coco Chanel

Pamper yourself!

When we're feeling stressed and anxious, it's easy to forget that pampering ourselves is an act of self-care. Indulging in feel-good pampering activities can promote relaxation and boost self-esteem and confidence – and that will help us approach life's challenges in a more positive frame of mind. Try out these pampering ideas!

- Get an appointment with a facialist for a skin-care consultation.

- Have a spontaneous wash and blow dry at a luxurious hair salon.

- Get a free makeover at a beauty counter.

- Indulge in a mani/pedi – just because you want to, and not because it's needed for a special occasion!

- Apply a hair mask and switch off while it sets to work.

🌿 Have a hot stone massage on a winter's day.

🌿 Try cryotherapy during the height of summer.

🌿 Give yourself a scalp massage.

🌿 Purchase a set of activewear to motivate you to work out.

🌿 Get a gait analysis done before investing in some good quality trainers.

🌿 Book a session with a personal trainer and set some fitness goals.

🌿 Open that bottle of posh bubble bath and wallow in the deepest bath you can run!

"Doing nothing has become one of the lost luxuries in these hectic times. But doing nothing, even for five minutes, can be rejuvenating."

Joan Marques

"Relaxation is the ultimate form of self-care. It is a gift we give ourselves to nurture our overall wellbeing."

Jess Connolly

Be your own best friend

Self-care is all about balance. Don't deprive yourself of things in the pursuit of better emotional or physical health, and don't set unrealistic targets. Sometimes, lying on the sofa and having a 10-minute daydream will be enough to make you feel rejuvenated.

If what you are doing doesn't make you feel better, it's far more productive to acknowledge this and move on than to keep slogging away at it! Imagine you're listening to someone explain that in trying to make changes for the better they ended up feeling worse, and then give yourself the same advice you would give them – just let it go!

Make what you want to do work around your resources, space and lifestyle: if an at-home fitness app suits you better than a gym membership, go for it! If you can't afford a holiday, plan some fun outings or day trips with friends. Be flexible, imaginative, and above all, be your own best friend.

Good luck!

"If you have the ability to love,

love yourself first."

Charles Bukowski